Understanding
The Charismatic Gifts

Understanding
The Charismatic Gifts

Father Peter B. Coughlin

Other books by Father Peter Coughlin

The Fire in My Heart

HE'S ALIVE!

Copyright © 1998 by Rev. Peter B. Coughlin, S.T.B., M.A.

3nd printing

Cover photograph by Sophie Riedemann

Published by:
C.C.S.O. Bread of Life Renewal Centre
www.thebreadoflife.ca

Printed and bound in Canada by:
Ave Maria Centre of Peace

ISBN 0-9683966-0-7

Acknowledgement

Sincere thanks to all who have encouraged me to write this book. May the fuller understanding of the Spirit's gifts be yours. A special thank you to Timeena Cervoni for her invaluable assistance in giving her time and effort to assist me, not only in the production and editing of this book, but for working with me, so that I may no longer be computer illiterate. God bless her and all of you who read and use this book for a greater understanding of the charismatic gifts.

Table Of Contents

Foreword
POWER WHEN THE SPIRIT COMES

We are a people most gifted by our God and yet we often do not recognize what has been given to us to teach and transform us, and to teach, transform and build up the Body of Christ, the Church. Empowered by the outpouring of the Holy Spirit from the days of Pentecost, all flesh can know and exercise the wondrous gifts of the Spirit of God.

All who open their hearts to the action of God's Spirit have all the gifts of the Spirit, not just a gift. Too many think that they are not favoured by God with even a gift because they are too unworthy, or too unintelligent, or are not good enough. And yet our God gifts all who say "Yes" to Him, all who ask, all who open their hearts to Him, all who desire to do His work, all who reach out to share what they have been given or have received from Him.

People who lived 2000 years ago were not much different than we are today. We still struggle, go through trials, try to overcome our weakness and our emptiness. But our God has given us the Isaian gifts to make us mighty in the Spirit of God, to know who we are in Christ and to have the strength to live the full Christian life as true disciples of Jesus. We receive these gifts at our Confirmation. We need only to understand what we have received and grow in these gifts.

When we give control of our lives to the Lord we receive what we call the baptism or the release of the Holy Spirit. From this point on we may begin to exercise the Corinthian gifts that are given by the Spirit for the building up and strengthening of the People of God, the Church.

Spiritual gifts are evident throughout the pages of Scripture, both in the Old and New Testaments. The Patriarchs of old such as Noah and Moses, the prophets, the judges, the apostles and disciples, all exercised gifts of the Holy Spirit of God, who is always active, always present, who only awaits the invitation to be active, to move freely.

At Pentecost we saw the Transformation of the apostles and disciples who went forth from the Upper Room as witnesses, joyfully and boldly proclaiming Jesus Christ as Lord. There was no doubt that Jesus had risen from the dead, that He was alive, that He had given them power from on high, the Spirit who was to remain with them. The Spirit came with power, gave power, prompted the proclamation of the Good News with power, with signs and wonders following.

The Church grew boldly and rapidly, because of the love and power evident in those who accepted Jesus as Lord. Countless numbers gave their lives for their faith in Jesus; the Church grew. Today, there is a fresh outpouring of the Spirit. Will you build the Church, renew the Church today by your acceptance of Jesus as Lord in your life? Will you let the Spirit of God work through you to build up the People of God? Will you not limit the Spirit of God, but have faith and be witnesses to the Truth?

Let there be a fresh outpouring of the Spirit today, tomorrow, and the next day, and the next and the next.

CHAPTER 1

USING YOUR GIFTS

"And he himself gave some men as apostles, and some as prophets and others again as evangelists, and others as pastors and teachers, in order to perfect the saints for a work of ministry, for building up the body of Christ, until we all attain to the unity of the faith and of the deep knowledge of the Son of God, to perfect manhood, to the mature measure of the fullness of Christ. And this he has done that we may now be, no longer children, tossed to and fro and carried about by every wind of doctrine devised in the wickedness of men, in craftiness, according to the wiles of error. Rather are we to practice the truth in love and so grow up in all things in him who is the head, Christ. For from him the whole body (being closely joined and knit together through every joint of the system according to the functioning in due measure of each single part) derives its increase to the building up of itself in love" (Ephes 4:11-16).

Paul names enthusiastically all that we have in common through Christ and through the work of the Holy Spirit.

Having so much in common is a call to union, love and peace.

There is still more: even particular gifts must be placed at the service of the community, in the same way as stones or bricks of a building. And what is being built is not just any building, nor is it simply a temple—it is the Body of Christ or the Perfect Man, made up of the millions of members now forming humanity and those of the future. Some day, when all are united, we will form this 'Perfect Human' with countless members.

Jesus of Nazareth lived humbly until His death, only once, but having been made the Head of humanity through His Resurrection, He suffers everywhere; He works in every field of human activity; He gives His life in every possible way; He gathers in Himself every form of love, and lives the whole diversity of human existence in the persons of His members.

He invites them to become a mature community, capable of being led by the truth, and of building itself up through love. We too should consider, to what degree, we have passed that age in which we needed the constant drive and direction of another. Spiritually speaking, adults are those who are conscious of their Christian responsibilities because they really know the love of God and are docile to the Spirit.

The Spirit of God graces us by His presence in a variety of ways not only for our own blessing but for the blessing of others. We are gifted as unique individuals, each having many gifts or manifestations of the Spirit's Presence within us, in order that our lives be directed on the Lord's path according to His unique plan for each of us, that we be strengthened and that we serve the People of God to meet their needs and build them up.

One group of these gifts is listed in Romans 12:6-8:

"Let each one of us, therefore, serve according to our different gifts. He, who by God's gift, is a prophet, let him say whatever faith inspires him to say. Let the deacon fulfil his office; let the teacher teach, and he who encourages, convince. You must, likewise, give with an open hand, preside with dedication, and be cheerful in your works of charity."

These are the gifts that, to some degree, are present in each of us although one or the other may predominate, making us have a particular motivating force or direction in our lives. To operate in the sphere of the gifts that are strong in us brings much joy into our lives. We may list these gifts as:

1. **Prophet or Perceiver**
   A person whose strong gift is being able to clearly recognize or perceive the Will of God. For this person, everything will look either right or wrong, good or bad, in tune with God's Will or out of it. This person would be a strong intercessor, having great faith that God answers prayer.

2. **Server or Doer of the Word**
   A person who really loves to serve others and is happiest doing so, being more a 'Martha' than a 'Mary.' Such a one would constantly notice opportunities to do things for others and would greatly manifest the gift of hospitality. Even this 'Martha' has great faith that whatever is started can be completed.

3. **Teacher**

   A person who loves to research and communicate the truth, especially the gospel message. This person searches for truth in everything, investigating so as to understand this truth and present it clearly. A person of faith who leads others to grasp and hold on to the truth.

4. **Encourager or Exhorter**

   A person who loves to encourage others to live in victory, one who moves others to achieve or accomplish or be what God calls them to be and do. This would be an extremely positive person who sees and responds to the opportunities to encourage people at whatever they do. As a person of faith, the encourager knows that every problem has a solution.

5. **Giver or Contributor**

   A person who loves to give time and talent, energy and means to benefit others and to respond to expressed needs that particularly advance the Kingdom of God. A person of faith who knows that God supplies every need and is willing to put himself and his resources at the service of others.

6. **Administrator, Facilitator or Leader**

   A person who loves to organize, lead or direct, knowing by faith, that any project can be accomplished by bringing together the right people to do it. As a person of broad vision, the administrator grasps the overall picture, sees all that is involved.

7. **Compassion Person or the One who shows Mercy**

   A person who responds to those in need by showing love

and compassion, care and charity. This person readily recognizes the hurts and wounds, the pain people experience, and reaches out to bring healing and love into action. As a person of faith, he can help others to work together in love.

While these gifts all exist to some degree, in all of us, our particular strengths are to interact with others that all the People of God may benefit, and together then, we cooperate with God's plans for our lives. By using our gifts for the glory of God and working together in mutual interdependence, we find our lives more and more fulfilled. Each gift is of equal value. No one is greater than another. In reality, we all minister in each area. We are each to perceive, serve, teach, exhort, contribute, lead and show mercy.

We read in Isaiah 11:2-3:

> "The Spirit of the Lord will rest upon him— a Spirit of wisdom and of understanding, a Spirit of counsel and of power, a Spirit of knowledge and of fear of the Lord—that he may rule in the fear of the Lord."

These are the gifts the Church focuses on during the Sacrament of Confirmation, gifts of strengthening the individual persons in their faith journey as they walk with Jesus through life.

1. **Wisdom**

   The spiritual state we arrive at when we become able to make judgments about everything in our lives because we have entered into a deep and personal relationship or union with God in love. St. Paul tells us that the one who has attained the gift of wisdom is "the spiritual person who judges all things" (1 Cor 2:15). Wisdom builds on the foundation of love. The more we love well, the more we grow in wisdom; the more we "put on Christ," the more we allow the Lord to make us who we are created to become—His disciples in deed and truth.

2. **Understanding**

The gift of the Spirit which enlightens us with divine truth so that with heart and mind we grasp the mysteries of God. With this gift, we not only see and understand the Lord more clearly, but we deeply appreciate the workings of God. We gain insight into the Scriptures, increased depth in prayer, appreciation of the sacraments, the action of God's grace, and our relationship with and growth in Him.

3. **Counsel**

Is hearing the 'small still voice' within us, the voice of the Lord telling us what to do. It is the gift of the Spirit that empowers us to make decisions in practical life situations through the Spirit's counsel or moment by moment direction in our lives.

4. **Power**

Also known as might, courage, strength and fortitude; it is the gift of the Spirit that enables us to face trials and dangers in the Christian faith-life with confidence and courage. This gift speaks of spiritual strength and holy boldness in sharing the gospel. In times of difficulty, this gift gives us the courage to go on, to overcome discouragement, to endure suffering, so that we come to full maturity in Christ Jesus, doing God's Will at all times.

5. **Knowledge**

   The gift of the Spirit that produces a deep certitude and trust in God that the truths of faith are accurate as He reveals them and we, through expectant faith, recognize God's action, His hand at work in all things. This gift produces absolute certitude: 'I know that I know that I know.' It is sure knowledge, without doubt.

6. **Piety or Fear of the Lord**

   That manifestation of the Holy Spirit within us that produces in us a loving and worshipful consciousness of God as our Father. This is called in Scripture, the "Spirit of adoption" (Rom 8:15). This gift brings us into a deep, loving, abiding relationship with God as our Father, Jesus as our Lord and Brother and the Holy Spirit as our Constant Companion who dwells within us. Through recognizing our relationship with the Blessed Trinity, we recognize that we share a real universal brotherhood/sisterhood with all of creation.

7. **Fear of the Lord or Reverence for the Lord**

   This gift is the doorway to a deeper spiritual life. It is the gift of the Holy Spirit that stirs within us a deep reverence and awe toward God which causes us to honour and obey Him. This gift helps us to overcome sin in our lives, honouring and obeying Him. Like humility, it helps us to see who God is and who we are.

   Another group of gifts listed in the New Testament are often called the manifestation gifts and are listed in

1 Corinthians 12:7-10 as gifts of service or ways in which the Spirit reveals His Presence in each one, as a particular manifestation. Paul writes to the Christians of Corinth to correct abuses, to teach, to bring good order into their community and in their meetings. We have all the gifts of the spirit operative in our midst as the need is present and the Spirit will operate through individuals in a variety of ways. When the community gathers, the Spirit will manifest Himself in different ways in different people.

1. **The Word of Wisdom**

   A revelation of wisdom beyond natural human wisdom that enables a person to know what to say or do. God's direction or wisdom is given to meet the need.

2. **The Word of Knowledge**

   A revelation of a word or information for a person or a situation that could not have been known by any natural means. It could be a revelation that reveals the secret thoughts or intent of a person, a word of healing or freedom being accomplished by the Lord, or simply God's diagnosis of a problem.

3. **Faith**

   The kind of wonder-working faith that can move mountains and waits expectantly for results. This kind of faith operates or is spoken without any doubt that it will be accomplished.

4. **Gift of Healing**

   The touch or move of God that brings about or speeds up a healing process. There are many different ways and varieties or degrees in which God manifests healing either spontaneously or in answer to prayer.

5. **Working Miracles**
   The demonstration of the power and action of God that goes beyond natural laws, as, for example, in instantaneous healing, in a sudden change of heart, or the supplying of something that is missing, e.g., the ability to see without eyes, to walk with a broken spinal cord, etc.

6. **Prophecy**
   The speaking forth of the mind and heart of God, to encourage, exhort, comfort, build up or strengthen. It is the appropriate Word of God being communicated to people at this particular time in this particular set of circumstances.

7. **Discerning of Spirits**
   The ability to judge through a situation to see what spirits are operative: the Holy Spirit, the evil spirit or the human spirit, or what combination of spirits. It is the ability to discern or see clearly the truth of the circumstances.

8. **Tongues**
   The prayer language given to a believer by the Holy Spirit but it has never been learned and is not known by the speaker. It is a love-language between the individual and the Lord in which the Spirit within expresses the prayer of praise, petition or deliverance. It is the ability to pray when we no longer know the words to say as we praise or intercede.

9. **Interpretation of Tongues**
   It is not translation but gives the sense of a message

spoken in tongues to the assembly. It may be inspired prayer or praise to God or a message similar to prophecy, that is able to capture the attention of the non-believer to recognize the presence of God. It may also reveal hidden things about a person's life or intentions.

Every disciple of Jesus has been given gifts and is to use them for the benefit of others. The gifts are God's action through us in the Holy Spirit to make the presence of God alive in us, revealing His love and power to all in need.

"Serve one another with the gifts each of you received, thus becoming good managers of the various graces of God. If you speak, deliver the Word of God; if you have a special ministry, let it be seen as God's power, so that in everything, God may be glorified in Jesus Christ." (1 Peter 4:10-11).

CHAPTER 2

THE ISAIAN GIFTS

"The spirit of the Lord shall rest upon him:
a spirit of wisdom and understanding, a spirit of
counsel and of strength, a spirit of knowledge
and of fear of the Lord, and His delight shall be
the fear of the Lord" (Is 11:2-3).

This is the source of the traditional names of the gifts of
the Holy Spirit. The Septuagint and the Vulgate sources read
"piety" for fear of the Lord in its first occurrence, thus
listing seven gifts. Pope Leo XIII in his encyclical, *Divinum
Illud*, said:

"By means of these seven gifts of the Holy
Spirit, the soul is furnished and strengthened so
as to be able to obey more easily and promptly
His voice and impulse."

Many people tend to evaluate themselves in terms of
how they are growing functionally in the use of charisms and
in terms of how they feel—the fruit of the Spirit being
viewed mainly as feelings. Having an incorrect perception,
people do not make solid, long term progress in terms of
their inner growth, and so their functional and emotional life
can suffer. Recognizing and cultivating the seven Isaian gifts
which deal with the inner transformation of the person can
foster a more healthy and balanced spiritual outlook.
Sometimes, people feel discouraged if they do not manifest
some of the more extraordinary charisms. The Isaian gifts are
given to all and are far more important than the Corinthian
gifts for the building up and growth of the individual.

Pope John Paul II teaches that the Second Vatican Council and the renewal that followed it, including the Charismatic Renewal, have as their purpose the enrichment of the faith. Each aspect of conciliar renewal is an enrichment of the Church. The complementary process of enrichment and integration must be taking place in all renewals of the Church, in the life of every individual.

Fear of the Lord is a gift of the Holy Spirit in which one has an attitude of reverence and awe toward God which causes one to honour and obey Him. Often, people are confused about this fear of the Lord and the emotion of fear. Fear of the Lord is not an emotion, but rather an attitude of reverence and awe towards God which causes one to honour Him and put Him first. Psalm 9:10 and Psalm 111:10 tell us that "the fear of the Lord is the beginning of wisdom." In 1 John 4:18, we read: "perfect love casts out fear." To grow in the fear of the Lord, we must recognize it, ask for it, meditate on God's great deeds in history, talk to Him carefully, attach great value to this gift, simply obey the Lord and follow Him. The great advantages of fear of the Lord are that it is the spiritual door to the full Christian life, a great aid in overcoming sin in our lives, enabling us to overcome worldly and carnal fears and bringing protection and blessing. "The angel of the Lord encamps around those who fear him" (Ps 34:7).

Strength (power, might, courage, fortitude) is the spiritual gift that enables us to face with strength and confidence the trials and dangers we encounter in the Christian life. In the Old Testament, references to this gift deal with fighting physical battles and accomplishing great earthly feats—for example, the battle of David and Goliath. In the New Testament, references deal with spiritual strength. In the Charismatic Renewal, this gift would be evident as a new boldness about sharing the Good News with others. It is seen often as the charismatic gift of evangelism. Also, it is seen as the overall strengthening of life in Christ and as an increase in one's ability to endure and persevere.

Strength is crucial to living in the Spirit, particularly when following the Lord becomes difficult. Too many weaken and grow discouraged on the journey. The sufferings we endure are used by the Lord to train and form us, and the cultivation of patience with regard to them enables the Lord to work more freely and quickly to bring us to maturity. To practice and cultivate the spirit of strength one must not give up and quit, one must do the Lord's will no matter how difficult, and do regular penances while reducing creature comforts.

Piety, called in Scripture "the spirit of adoption" (Rm 8:15), is that manifestation of the Spirit which produces in us a loving and worshipful consciousness of God as our Father. This is a very common part of the charismatic experience and affects us in a very deep level of our inner being. It is a profound sense of filial closeness. Piety leads us to a true image of our Father as merciful, faithful, abounding in steadfast love, slow to anger, but also firm and just. We grow in piety through the practice of justice, a general attitude of cooperation with authority in every area of our lives, with material things, reputation, religious obligations, as family members and citizens. Truthfulness and friendliness must be cultivated. The effect of piety is the spirit of filial relationship with God and brotherhood with all.

Counsel is the gift that empowers us to make decisions in the Spirit in practical life situations. After the Baptism in the Holy Spirit, we begin to hear the voice of the Lord telling us what to do. The gift of counsel is good common sense and allows for levels of maturity as we grow in Christian maturity. We may approach words from the Lord by distinguishing between prophecies and counsels, with the understanding that counsels are far more common than prophecies and more foundational to living the Christian life. This will give us greater freedom in the Spirit.

Prudence is the application of sound reason to practical action and is a virtue highly prized in the Scriptures. Counsel is a great help in overcoming many of the common obstacles in the spiritual life—for example, scrupulosity and rigidity . It is essential to effective leadership in the Body of Christ. To cultivate this gift, remain humble, recognize your weakness and dependence on Him to make the right choices in His time and way. Sustain a personal prayer life as a must in order to always remain alert to the voice of the Lord and His guidance.

Knowledge is the gift of the Spirit that produces in us a deep trust and sureness about the Lord and about the truths of Christian revelation. This gift plays a key role in the initial phase of life in the Spirit because it gives certitude about God's revelation of Himself and His Word. After Baptism in the Spirit, faith is radically different from previous understanding. We learn that faith is a total personal trust in the Lord without reservation and is applicable to everything in our lives. To cultivate this gift, it is important to develop expectant faith which is a firm foundation for growth. Hold fast to Christian truth, both in Scripture and tradition. Look for the Lord's hand in all things and constantly guard against worldly wisdom while cultivating a spirit of detachment from life on earth.

Understanding is the gift of the Spirit which enlightens our minds and hearts with divine truth so that we can grasp the mysteries of the Lord. Understanding enables us to see the Lord more clearly while wisdom shows us what He wants us to do. Baptism in the Spirit effects a strong outpouring of the gift of understanding. Very common signs of this are new insight into the Scriptures, increased depth in prayer and renewed appreciation of the sacraments. These are commonly told as fruits of the Charismatic Renewal, but they are the fruit of understanding. This gift helps us to appreciate the gift of tongues and helps us to grasp the meaning of the whole Charismatic Renewal. Growing in this gift leads us through repentance and enlightenment to unification in which we seek the Lord for His sake alone.

Wisdom is the spiritual state we arrive at when we become able to make judgments about everything in our lives on the basis of a deep, personal union with the Lord in love. 1 Corinthians 2:15 tells us: "The spiritual person who judges all things is one who has attained the gift of wisdom." Christian spirituality sees wisdom as love which has been perfected and supernaturalized by the full presence of the Spirit in the soul. Love is the foundation on which wisdom is built. For those in the Renewal, love is self-expressive, freeing, spontaneous, easy, a foretaste of what is to be when we reach full maturity in Christ Jesus.

We are told in Proverbs to make wisdom our first priority, to get it, beg for it—just get it. Wisdom cannot be attained by our own efforts—the Lord must give it to us. He will give it if we ask. Associate with those who are already wise and listen to their words of training and correction. Learn to see yourself as a gift of ministry to others. If we are to become wise, we must "put on love"—the foundation on which wisdom is built.

CHAPTER 3

THE WORD OF WISDOM

The word of wisdom is one of the teaching gifts listed in 1 Corinthians 12. It is a manifestation of God's presence, power and wisdom. In great part, the New Testament is made up of utterances of wisdom and knowledge, inspired teaching and preaching.

The spiritual gift of a word of wisdom is the action of the Holy Spirit in a given moment to meet a specific situation or need a person may have. It is the Lord's direction on how to resolve a problem that has been identified through a word of knowledge or a prophecy. This gift, as others of the "manifestation gifts," is a passing manifestation of the Spirit to help or heal or bring clarity to a given situation. It comes as divine insight, telling us what to do in the present need.

This is not merely normal human wisdom, although that is highly prized and can be greatly beneficial in any circumstance. But when one does not know how to proceed, the Holy Spirit gives the insight in prayer.

We are told in 1 Corinthians 1:24 that "Christ is the wisdom of God." In the Wisdom books of the Old Testament we find much spiritual wisdom and we are admonished to get wisdom, whatever the cost. James 1:5 says: "If any of you lacks wisdom, he should ask God and it will be given to him."

In my own experience, I have sensed the Lord giving me a word of wisdom to answer a particular question or help provide a solution to a given problem. I know the word has come directly from the Lord and I've been amazed that I've said things I didn't even know. Sometimes it comes as a new insight by which I understand something clearly that was obscure before, or that I did not know. This, at times, can be a word of knowledge; at other times, it is a word of wisdom, or both. The wisdom uses the knowledge, applying it in the circumstances.

In the Old Testament we have Solomon known for his wisdom and understanding. He had prayed: "Give your servant an understanding heart to govern your people, that I may discern between good and evil" (1 Kgs 3:9). A famous example of his use of the gift of wisdom was to resolve the claims of two women for the same child. Through the word of knowledge Solomon recognized the true mother, and with the word of wisdom he was able to publicly solve the question of parentage.

Many times Jesus manifested this wisdom through the parables He spoke. He could answer His accusers easily over questions about His authority—paying taxes to Caesar, sending Peter out fishing to pay the temple tax, and many others. All were amazed at His wisdom, knowledge and power.

The word of wisdom shows one how to apply the words of knowledge or revelation that have been given. It is a valuable gift when praying for healing or in the inner healing ministry. This wisdom can help to avoid dangers, help one to speak rightly and correctly in difficult circumstances, and it causes people to be amazed and to give glory to God.

God gives this gift through the Holy Spirit and we should ask for it as we ask God for His other gifts.

This is also seen as a teaching gift, a special inspiration by which the Lord works through one person to give understanding to others, or perhaps a special word of advice or instruction. This word of wisdom is concerned with the best way to live as a Christian. For example, in Mark 10:20, Jesus gives advice to the rich young man to go and sell all he has and give it to the poor, then to come and follow Him. Wisdom is also evident clearly at the Council of Jerusalem when Peter said that the Gentiles should not have to follow the full Mosaic law when they became Christians. Much of what St. Paul says in 1 Corinthians chapters 12 to 14 are examples of the utterance of wisdom—practical, spiritual teaching.

Natural understanding is acquired by study. Inspired understanding from the Lord feeds the human spirit in a way that natural understanding cannot, because it is a manifestation of the Spirit in a person. It makes a deep change in people, giving them a heightened spiritual life. When one is open to the Lord's direction, he can learn as much as the person being spoken to and know things that he has never studied or thought through.

How does one exercise the gift of the word of wisdom? One should be striving to be in a right, open and prayerful relationship with the Lord. The one who speaks the gift is given a spiritual revelation and this could happen in a variety of ways as the person receives a mental image or picture, a word, a prompting to speak, an inner voice, a sense of what

God would say. My own experience has been of beginning to speak, with a prompting, and then being amazed to recognize it ás a word of wisdom. This word may also be given as a prophecy or be part of a prophetic preaching or teaching. The gift comes in the moment of need as one turns to the Lord, and as we are told in the Scriptures, "the Spirit will give us the words to speak in that hour" (Lk 21:15).

In the healing ministry this gift can be invaluable because it becomes clear how one should respond or act, pray or minister to the ones receiving prayer or counselling. Frequently, this gift is exercised in the Sacrament of Reconciliation, pointing direction, giving clarity, showing how to act or respond.

Those receiving the ministry of the word should be able to recognize the direct word of the Lord on how to proceed and be able to do so in a positive, loving and wise way. Blessings are received by those who are seeking the ministry: God is glorified, people are amazed, and help, healing and understanding or freedom of some kind should be the direct result of the word of wisdom being ministered.

Love is the first fruit of the Spirit (Ga 5:22). They go together—wisdom in the understanding, and love in the heart. One does not acquire wisdom unless one loves. The more one loves, the more wisdom is produced.

In 1 Corinthians, chapters 1 to 3, wisdom is mentioned twenty-four times, and always with a marked distinction between "wisdom of men" and the "wisdom of God." Paul deliberately puts aside his own wisdom that he might be a channel for the supernatural wisdom of the Spirit (1 Cor 2:1-4).

In Paul, the word of wisdom is the preaching of Christ and His cross and those things which God has prepared for those who love Him. This would be recognized as the kind of preaching in which our hearts burn within us.

In the Acts, the apostles give us a wonderful example of the word of wisdom in action. The twelve dealt with the daily problems of ministry in looking after the widows and orphans by choosing seven men filled with the Holy Spirit and faith to minister while they themselves focused on prayer and the proclamation of the word (Ac 6:1-7). Their answer to the situation shows that they were committed to the highest spiritual principles, while at the same time embracing what made perfect common sense. The result was that the whole community was pleased and edified and many were added to their numbers as a result.

CHAPTER 4

THE WORD OF KNOWLEDGE

"All the treasures of Wisdom and Knowledge are hidden in Christ" (Col 2:3). A Word of Knowledge is God's revelation, through the Holy Spirit, of facts about a person or a situation that God chooses to reveal for His own purposes. The purpose could be for healing, freedom, blessing, correction, warning of dangers or wrong attitudes, to clarify a situation or to provide direction. Basically, a Word of Wisdom tells us what to do with the knowledge received.

A Word of Knowledge or Revelation does not give secret knowledge so as to control a person or situation; nor does it indicate that the one who receives the word has access to special revelations from the Holy Spirit for the purpose of giving direction to others on how to live their lives, or what decisions they are to make. Words of Knowledge do not give new revelation of God, since all must conform to the revealed truth of the Sacred Scriptures. The knowledge given by the Spirit is for the purpose of blessing or being of benefit to those for whom the word is intended. This is not mere human knowledge or intuition, but is a direct gift through the Spirit of God to help the person or the situation, whether the knowledge imparted deals with the past, present and/or future.

There are many biblical examples of the Word of Knowledge in operation. Among them would be disclosing hypocrisy (2 Kg 5:20-27), calling the Samaritan woman to conversion (Jn 4: 18-19, 29), indicating a person's need

(Ac 9:11), revealing the source of corruption within the early church community (Ac 5:3), insight into the hearts and thoughts of others (Jn 2:24), the location of the coin in the fish's mouth (Mt 17:27), telling Peter that a visitor would come (Ac 10:17-23). Such words may be given to disclose, warn, prepare, provide, encourage, build up, increase faith, to meet a particular need or to give understanding of the person or situation. Such revelation may also bring repentance, give guidance or direction.

This word from the Lord may come as a thought, a word, a sense, or through an emotion. It should bear fruit in testimony when it is the means of bringing about healing or the acceptance of healing, deeper faith, a renewed life, joy, a greater outpouring or experience of the Father's love. It may also bring strength or power beyond a person's capabilities—help a person to praise God or to proclaim Jesus as Lord.

This gift of the Holy Spirit at work in us is far more common than we may think. We exercise this gift often in a very natural way in a whole variety of experiences. For example, when at the prayer meeting we may know what will be sung next, or who will speak next, or what the next word will be. Themes or teachings inspired by the Lord may come to mind as if knowing exactly the need of the moment. The Lord may reveal a particular ministry for a person. Frequently we may hear the word for healing or freedom, or to meet a particular need of someone at the prayer meeting. A particular passage of Scripture may come to mind and we read it and it meets the need of another individual or the group.

This word may be given also in the selection of leaders, prayer partners, or to find lost objects (usually St. Anthony is invoked). I remember being in Ireland once on a bus tour when it was discovered that a woman's purse was missing. My response (a Word of Knowledge) was that it was in her bag under the bus, and then I prayed: "St. Anthony, get it there; I don't care how you do it." When the bus stopped she checked her bag and her purse was there. Praise God!

How does one receive this gift? God gives His gifts, just as He determines (cf. 1 Cor 12:11). We may ask for the gift that we may be of help to others in ministry. We may receive it from another who disciples us in the ministry, by an impartation of the Spirit's power and presence. Some are used regularly in the exercise of this gift; others may use it on occasion in ministering to another person. Certainly the gift should be encouraged. It is also good to expect it as the Lord's provision and exercise it accordingly with prudence and discretion. We do need to be careful about not embarrassing another and not breaking another's trust or invading their privacy. Sometimes the Word of Knowledge is given not to be spoken out but to guide us in how to pray.

The Word of Knowledge may be received or seen as in a vision or dream or picture that seems to be somehow superimposed over a person's face or the afflicted area of the body. The word may be heard clearly with our ears, or strongly in our heart. A person may receive the word as a sense of pain or hurt in the body—a pain that is suddenly present and that indicates the condition of another. Usually when it is spoken out, the pain disappears in both the one for whom the word is given and the one who speaks the word. There could also be a sense of the power of God present in a significant way or by a strong awareness of heat or tingling in the hands, indicating we should lay on hands for healing. The word comes in a whole variety of ways: sometimes seen, heard, felt, read, said, or just known.

When the word is given to a person we should not try to interpret it but rather allow the person receiving it to interpret it. Nor should we speak the word in inner healing or prayer ministry if it will hurt or cause embarrassment. It may be better to ask a question that allows freedom to the recipient's response. For example: don't ask if your father abused you; but rather more appropriate would be, "At about the age of nine did you have a traumatic experience?"

We should always look to the fruit to help discern the movement of the Spirit. Is faith increased? Did healing occur? Were blessings received? Were blocks removed? Was God glorified? The Word of Knowledge is certainly part of normal Christian life in Jesus Christ. It is necessary in inner healing ministry, enables the ministry of Jesus to continue through us, and points out blocks or barriers, areas of resistance to God's love. Frequently, this gift is used in counselling, prayer therapy, and reconciliation or confession. It even has an evangelical effect, as the Samaritan woman who said to the people in her town: "Come and see a man who has told me everything I have ever done" (Jn 4:25).

The Word of Knowledge gives a spiritual diagnosis from the Lord of a person's problem; whereas the Word of Wisdom tells us what to do with the word received. With all the gifts of the Holy Spirit, it is important to study and understand them, to pray for them in the community and to ask the Lord to exercise them through you.

One last note: when Words of Knowledge are spoken out at a prayer meeting or healing Mass, it is good to look for a response—for people to confirm the word(s). Otherwise, if words are given and no one responds, faith is not built up or increased and the one who spoke is not confirmed in ministry. We do need to be aware of the human condition: fear of embarrassment, wanting time to check it out, etc. I remember once, years ago, announcing a healing in someone's left ankle to a congregation of about 500. No one responded and I said it three times. I thought: "I'll never do this again!" The following week, three people phoned to tell me their left ankle was healed. Praise God!

CHAPTER 5

FAITH AND SURRENDER

By faith a person completely submits or surrenders their intellect and will to God. Faith requires a response and so to obey in faith is to submit freely to the word of God that has been heard. Abraham, for all of us, is the "Father of all believers," a model of real obedience to the word of God which he received in faith. We recognize the Blessed Virgin Mary as the perfect embodiment of faith who, by her "fiat," her "yes," became the mother of the Messiah. Certainly the Scriptures are rich in witnesses to faith. "Faith is the assurance of things hoped for, the conviction of things not seen" (Heb 11:1).

The Father gives the grace of believing in His son Jesus, who is "the author and perfecter of our faith" (Heb 12:2), to all of us who recognize that He is indeed the Son of God who came into our world that we "might have life and have it to the full" (Jn 10:10). Elizabeth says of her cousin, Mary: "Blessed is she who believed" (Lk 1:45). Throughout her life Mary's faith never wavered.

Faith is first of all a personal adherence of a person to God, but it is also a free assent to the whole Truth revealed by God. As a personal adherence to God and an assent to His Truth, Christian faith differs from the faith we put in any human person. It is right to entrust oneself wholly to God and to believe absolutely and completely what He reveals. For a Christian then, believing in God cannot be separated from believing in the One He sent, His beloved Son, in whom the Father is well pleased. God tells us to listen to

Him. "For God so loved the world that he sent his only Son that whoever believes in him may not be lost but may have eternal life" (Jn 3:16).

One cannot believe in Jesus Christ without sharing in His Spirit, because it is the Holy Spirit who reveals to mankind who Jesus is. For no one can say "Jesus is Lord" except by the Holy Spirit. No one comprehends the thoughts of God except the Spirit of God, who is God himself, Third Person of the Blessed Trinity.

Faith is a grace, a gift of God, a supernatural virtue given through baptism. Each one needs the interior helps of the Holy Spirit who moves the heart, converting it to God who opens the mind to accept and believe the Truth. Faith is something we exercise only by grace and the interior move of the Spirit. Faith is more certain than all human knowledge because it is founded on God's word and He cannot lie or deceive. Always, faith seeks understanding. St. Augustine wrote: "I believe, in order to understand; and I understand, the better to believe."

Faith is a personal act, a free response of the human heart to the initiative of God who reveals Himself. Faith is caught; it cannot really be taught. We may learn about faith, but it is a divine light that illuminates God's revelation within the heart and mind of one who embraces Truth. We may profess the Truths of faith through the Apostles' or the Nicene Creeds, either individually or as part of community. Faith is very personal, yet at the same time it is what binds a believing community together. In Baptism we ask for faith from the Church, knowing that faith offers us eternal life.

The Church's role is to faithfully guard the faith and hand it on intact from generation to generation.

Faith is necessary for salvation. "He who believes and is baptized will be saved; but he who does not believe will be condemned" (Mk 16:16). The faith we embrace leads us to surrender, abandonment, entrustment, to giving God permission, to stepping beyond ourselves, beyond the limits we see. Faith leads to trust that God provides, looks after every detail, desires only our good, and so faith leads us to surrender to God's leading, His way. "For I know well the plans I have in mind for you, says the Lord, plans for your welfare, not for woe! Plans to give you a future full of hope" (Jer 19:11). It's worth it for us to bring all of our life under the Lordship of Jesus, to let Him be Lord, to choose His terms not ours.

If we would choose to cultivate a fertile environment for the Holy Spirit to work sovereignly in our lives, then we need to learn to obey every prompting He gives us. We know there is no controlling the Spirit of God since He moves or blows as He wills—whether in the mighty sound of raging wind or as a still, quiet voice within. Sin grieves or saddens the Holy Spirit, so we must keep our hearts clean or free of sin. The practice of regular confession will help us to maintain clean hearts through which the Holy Spirit can work.

By faith we invite the presence of the Holy Spirit to come into our lives. "Through him we are fully confident that whatever we ask, according to his will, he will grant us" (1 Jn 5:14). We already know that it is His will that we be filled with the Holy Spirit (Eph 5:18). With great confidence we are able to pray "Come Holy Spirit, fill our lives!" We must not only thirst after the Holy Spirit (Jn 7:37), but we must walk with the Spirit. "If we live by the Spirit, let us be led by the Spirit" (Gal 5:25). We need to know the Word of God and cultivate a sensitivity to the still, small voice of God speaking His direction to us (Jn 10:14). As disciples, we must make ourselves available to the Holy Spirit through obedience to His Word, to do what the Lord says and to be in the right place at the right time. When we surrender to Jesus, put our faith in Him, He baptizes us in the Holy Spirit.

He works in and through Scripture, life's circumstances, prayer time, and Christian fellowship to bring us to a fullness of faith. Our spiritual growth comes about as a product of the initiating, empowering work of the Holy Spirit and our active cooperation with Him. To grow, we need both divine initiative and our active response to the move and prompting of the Spirit. God's Word has the power to teach, introduce clear thinking, inform our consciences, conform our lives to the standards of God (1 Tm 3:16); protect us against sin (Ps 119:11) and bring freedom (Ps 119:45). It certainly is critical for our spiritual growth in faith that we act on what God's word speaks to us, or our belief and knowledge are not authentic, because faith is active not passive. If we believe the Lord, then we do what He says.

Faith is characterized by people believing God's word regardless of their personal circumstances. When our faith is informed, then we put our trust in the Lord who overcame the cross, the most evil circumstance in all history.

The gift of faith expressed by St. Paul in his first letter to the Corinthians is a supernatural surge of confidence from the Holy Spirit which surges within a person faced with a particular situation or need. The person has an absolute certainty and assurance that God is about to act through a word or action. This utterance may be blessing or cursing, an alteration or removal. It may even be a creation or destruction. Not only is it the certain knowledge of God's intervention at a certain point or in a given situation, but it is also the authority to bring about this intervention through the Holy Spirit's power.

We look at faith as the doctrine we profess, or as a basic trust in God for salvation, or as a gift of the Holy Spirit, or as a fruit of the Spirit we call faithfulness.

St. James speaks of the prayer of faith that can heal the sick and Jesus speaks of faith as a mustard seed that can move mountains. Daniel by faith is preserved from danger in the lions' den, the three young men in the fiery furnace are not harmed, Elijah is fed by the ravens, the son of the woman of Zarephath by the faith of Elijah is restored to life. Faith is operative for Abraham and Sarah when Sarah bears a son in her old age. The gift of faith enabled the Israelites, as long as Moses held up his hands, to win the battle against the Amalekites at Rephidim.

The scriptures are full of such workings of the gift of faith. I've seen it several times in the multiplication of food; and frequently, throughout the course of history, in the lives of people of faith, the gift of faith has been operative to resolve all kinds of domestic, financial and spiritual problems. In the New Testament, Jesus did many things by faith: sending Peter to catch the fish with a coin in its mouth in order to pay the temple tax; Jesus cursing the fig tree that it not bear fruit any more; Jesus raising Lazarus, calling him out of the tomb after he had been dead four days.

Not only is God glorified, but faith is increased; people are amazed at God's interventions in answer to the word of faith; and people come to faith in Jesus Christ. The gifts also work together, and several gifts may operate at the same time. For example, I remember some years ago, while holidaying with friends, that an eight-year-old son who was helping the woman next door had a dangerous encounter. He went to the woodshed to get something and when he opened the door, he broke a large wasps' nest and was swarmed and stung many, many times. When I turned and saw what was happening I simply, without thinking, said aloud: "In Jesus' name be gone!" The wasps literally disappeared. The boy was brought into the house and prayed with for healing. In ten minutes he was calmly eating his lunch with no apparent ill effects, though he had been stung dozens of times. Here I saw the gifts of faith, healing and miracle all working together. And so it is for all of us as we become people "full of faith and the Holy Spirit," people surrendered to the Lord in the way of faith.

CHAPTER 6

HEALING: THE MASTER'S TOUCH

An important part of the work of Jesus in the world today is in the area of healing. The Church has re-discovered in our own day the power of God, real and active, touching hearts and lives the world over. Since Vatican II the Sacrament of the Anointing of the Sick has been given new emphasis in the Church. The Charismatic Renewal has brought about a new emphasis on healing and expectant faith. Jesus is alive, touching people and making them whole through the power of the Holy Spirit. Once, healing seemed to be found only in the realm of saints and shrines where the sick recovered health, gained strength and courage, peace and the acceptance of God's will in their lives.

Still today there are many and varied attitudes towards healing: God doesn't heal people, we have to suffer, this is too little or too big for the Lord to be bothered, God heals everything if you have enough faith, only a saint can heal, healing is a rare exception, there are no miracles today—and so it goes. But God is far more active than many expect. His ways and timing are in the Divine Will and He doesn't need anyone to tell Him what to do or how or when. But we can freely turn to Him for the grace of healing in whatever our needs may be.

Jesus is the healer. There is no other. Even healings that come to us through Mary and the saints are through their intercession with Jesus the Healer. Healing is given as a manifestation of the Holy Spirit to build up, encourage, strengthen, make new or whole an individual or a group for the glory of God and the blessing of His people. Every healing has a purpose: to sanctify or to make holy the recipient, to glorify God, to build faith, to be a sign of the power and presence of God, to meet the need, to change the circumstances, to build up the Church.

Healing may be physical, psychological, emotional, spiritual, relational. It may be healing of memories or hurts in the past, or freeing one in the present to move on in the future. Whenever healing is asked or prayed for, healing occurs, though it may not be what is asked. For example, a person asking healing for the back may discover a knee problem is healed. A person seeking healing for an arthritic condition may discover tremendous peace as resentments disappear. Every human being has a real need for healing in their lives in order to enter fully into God's will. It's true that the Lord loves us as we are, but He loves us too much to leave us where we are. He heals us and sets us free from bondage that we may be better agents of His love and mercy, witnesses to His love and power, and members who are actively involved in the faith community. Healings remind us of God's loving presence and are a source of joy to all.

The Lord works through the medical profession, through medicine and prayer. It's always good to pray over the medication we take that it may be the blessing it is meant to be. The Lord also works sovereignly according to the Father's will, either healing gradually, in a speeded up way, or instantaneously. Healing certainly is a mystery that involves the plan of God, the purpose of the infirmity or sickness, expectant faith, the need of the community or person involved, the lesson one needs to learn through the infirmity, the right timing, the glory of God, and the readiness to receive. Our attitudes certainly play a great part in the mystery. Sometimes healing comes completely unexpectedly. At other times we may struggle with "not being healed."

We may pray for healing at any time, but it is best to first ask the Lord what His will is in each particular case and then to pray accordingly. Some needs presented in prayer first require a decision on the part of the one in need; for example, where one is dealing with addiction, alcoholism, sinful sexual relationships. When the decision to be free is made, then prayer may be intensely powerful because the grace given has the opportunity to work in the individual's life. There may also need to be secondary decisions made: for example, to change one's living place, companions, recreation time, etc.

In the New Testament we see abundant healings in the ministry of Jesus. "And all who touched him were made well" (Mk 6:56). Jesus communicated His power to heal to His apostles even before Pentecost, as a sign that the Kingdom of God is at hand. Even after Pentecost, the healings were so numerous that even the shadow of Peter (Ac 5:15), and the handkerchiefs or cloths touched to Paul (Ac 19:12) brought them about. In the early Church we see how common healing is, as people are encouraged to send for the elders to pray over the sick (Jas 5:14-15). Healings and preaching are closely connected. Healings confirm the word that is preached, in Jesus' day and in our own. Jesus had great compassion for people. He taught, fed and healed them. Today, He still carries on this ministry through those who are compassionate, sensitive, loving and bold enough to reach out with His power.

Through the Church, healing is the basis of the Sacraments of Eucharist, Baptism, Reconciliation, and Anointing of the Sick. Jesus heals, sets free, graces and blesses His people with His power and His love, drawing them into holiness and righteousness of life. He renews and makes whole the inner life that is made manifest in the external dimensions of who we are.

Very often the experience of healing takes place in the context of the prayer meeting, healing Mass, or a conference where expectant faith is present, a number of people gather, and praise is strong. Some are gifted by God with a ministry of healing to an exceptional degree, some have their "specialties" such as backs, knees, cancer, etc. Some, you could say, are "general practitioners." Some minister regularly as part of a team, others individually, and at other times the whole community that has gathered together prays for a particular need. In an atmosphere of praise and worship, love and compassion, expectant faith asks the Lord in His goodness to meet the needs of those suffering or in pain. Remember, though, that God works through whoever says "yes" to Him and anyone and everyone then can pray for healing to take place. A "special" healer or a "particular prayer team" has no corner on the market where the ministry of Jesus is concerned. The apostle James (5:16) tells us that "the prayer of the upright man has great power, provided he perseveres."

To pray for inner healing or the healing of memories usually takes a number of appointments in which a team prays through the life of an individual from conception to the present day. Most often these inner healing ministry teams focus on the childhood experiences in seeking to bring healing to root causes. But there is much trauma in adult life circumstances that also need effective ministry of healing. Many self-help groups do wonderful work, but we still need the touch of the Master to bring wholeness to the afflicted areas of our lives so that the transition into holiness and righteousness of life may be made.

Healing is often accompanied with the gift of tears—a wonderful gift described by one of the saints as the "washing of the soul." Tremendous release may accompany healing as a burden is lifted, a person set free, tension is lifted, anxiety dispelled, painful memories let go, forgiveness given or accepted.

Joy is another indicator of healing taking place, as is peace and a new sense of the presence of God, His personal love and power. Indeed, healing is the Master's touch. Let Him touch you; ask and expect much!

CHAPTER 7

MIRACLES

A miracle is a direct intervention by the power of the Holy Spirit in the natural order through an individual who prays or speaks out a word of command to change the existing situation or circumstances. Among the events that could be classed as miracles would be the instant healing of a serious disease, the sudden conversion or concession of an enemy of the Church, a complete change of heart or mind by one in authority, the sudden arrival or removal of persons under divine influence so that a particular need is met or a problem solved.

Many question whether it would be a coincidence or a special act of divine intervention. But for Catholics who are not to be superstitious or worldly-minded, there is only God-incidence—that is, they recognize the hand of God at work in every circumstance of daily life. And sometimes God works in miraculous ways, whether they be in large or small matters.

We are familiar with the fact that the working of miracles needs to take place for the beatification and canonization of saints. For the founder of a community, the first miracle is recognized in the actual founding of a new order or society, since that is already a miraculous undertaking and achievement. We also recognize miracles at holy sites such as Lourdes and Guadeloupe. And we also recognize them through holy people such as Mother Teresa who not only founded new communities but also daily brought life and healing to many of the world's poor.

The Lord often bestows miracles to encourage, strengthen and support the faith of His people or to correct a given situation which cannot be accomplished by any natural means. Miracles may also be given to show God's power at work in response to a ministry of preaching or teaching. A miracle brings about awe and wonder at God's power so that glory is given to God. Amazement and new or strengthened faith is often the result.

Jesus worked miracles because of the great compassion and mercy He had for His people to meet their needs, whether it was changing water into wine (the very first of His signs), walking on water, calming the storm, feeding the multitudes who had no food, or raising the dead to life. Jesus and the apostles worked signs and wonders to extend the Kingdom of God, to give faith in Jesus, to confirm His power and authority. When the Kingdom is preached, God's power is revealed.

When we study the Scriptures we see the purpose for miracles, whether it was to confirm the word preached (Ac 13:11-12), to deliver God's people from danger (Ac 12:4-11), to raise the dead (Jn 11:38-44), to display the power of God (Ps 145:3-7), to provide for those in need (Mk 6:13, 30-44), or to carry out the judgment of God as in the plagues on Egypt (Ex 7-11), or with Ananias and Sapphira (Ac 13:11-12).

This tremendous power of God is seen throughout the Scriptures, yet the Old Testament does not speak of miracles since no word for miracle existed in Hebrew. Moses, Elijah, Elisha all exercized miraculous power.

St. Paul lists the working of miracles among the charisms of the Holy Spirit. Works of power, signs and wonders designate the direct intervention of the God of all history. Jesus felt power flowing out of Him (Mk 5:30). Luke records the promise of Jesus that His Church would be "clothed with power from on high" (Lk 24:29). We see the miracles of Philip in Samaria (Ac 8:6), the raising of Dorcas from the dead (Ac 9:36-43), the blinding of Elymas (Ac 13:11), the raising of Eutychus from the dead (Ac 20:10), Paul's health even after he was bitten by a poisonous snake (Ac 28:5). In Galatians 3:5, Paul speaks of God working miracles among them.

So often the charisms work together, such as faith, healing and miracles. It's hard to say where one leaves off and the other begins. Faith and miracles are closely connected. Miracles are more common than we expect because they cover many different situations, not just healing. Miracles are a much more powerful sign of God's presence and action than healings. Healings may be instantaneous, gradual, or speeded up recovery; whereas, miracles happen instantaneously in every case, as God's power goes forth in response to the spoken word. To change the circumstances, to bring complete healing in the moment is certainly miraculous. Faith certainly has to be involved as one speaks the word of command in Jesus' name without doubt and with full certitude and expectant faith.

But, God, of course, can move sovereignly in a situation in response to prayer without the word of command spoken in faith. After all, He is the God of the impossible as well as the possible.

Very frequently, miracles occur at the beginning of a faith walk when an individual turns to the Lord and He responds by giving an unforgettable experience or sign of His love, His power and fidelity. As an individual grows more in the spiritual life, drawing closer to the Lord in a life of prayer, service and faith, God may grant other miracles. After all, as James tells us "the prayer of the upright man has great power" (Jas 5:16). So the more we draw near to Him, the more the presence and power of the Spirit becomes evident, and one of the ways is through miracles. An active faith and a real love for God's people expressed in compassion for them and with real trust in the Lord is the necessary seed-bed for miracles to occur. The one who calls forth the miracle needs to be sensitive to the Lord's promptings, grasp His Will in the moment and then needs to yield to the power of God moving in the heart or the need of the moment.

Miracles are most often seen as the Lord's confirmation of a preaching gift where Jesus Christ is proclaimed and revealed. The preacher, of course, needs to live his faith in Jesus. Miracles may remove obstacles to God's will and are certainly present in the lives of those who have matured in the Spirit. The age of miracles is still among us and will be in an even greater way. After all, it has been prophesied that an age of great glory is coming for the Church when God will move in power with great signs and wonders. Many look to a time of great tribulation and make that their focus rather than looking to the mighty move of God in power and authority to defeat the darkness and bring light to a lost world.

Miracles occur only when there is no possible way by our own efforts to bring about the needed objective— whether it be a healing or a change in circumstances. Prayer and expectant faith avail much.

We do not know how God works miracles, but He does. Every person and every prayer group, every family, I'm sure, can recount the unexplainable in their lives. When we look back at the circumstances or events of our lives we can see where God has been mightily at work. With the eyes of faith we recognize His miraculous touch. We can never demand a miracle or tell God what He must do, but as we are sensitive to His prompting we may be commissioned by Him to command the miracle to take place in Jesus' name.

Compassion or anger may precipitate the miraculous move of God. Faith that this is God's will in this moment, accompanied by an absolute conviction that what is needed will occur, allows the miracle worker to speak the word or perform the action that effects the miracle. We see this as Jesus heals the deaf and dumb man, putting His fingers in his ears and spittle on his tongue. He spoke the word "be opened," and the man could hear and speak clearly. The people were completely astonished and said, "He has done all things well; he makes the deaf hear and the dumb speak" (Mk 7:31-37).

What are the miracles God has worked in your life? How has Jesus used you to work miracles in the lives of others?

CHAPTER 8

CALLED TO BE PROPHET

In the call of Jeremiah (1:4-19) we hear how he is set apart and appointed as prophet to the nations by the Lord God. The young man claims that he is too young, that he does not know how to speak. But the Lord God touches Jeremiah, placing His words in the young man's mouth. The young man is moved by the Spirit and will obey the Lord, whatever the risks involved and in spite of the resistance of his timid nature. Jeremiah hears God repeating the word He spoke to Moses: "I am with you to rescue you" (Ex 3:12), the same word He speaks to Paul (Ac 26:17).

The mission of Jeremiah is one he finds frightening, yet the Lord assures him: "Before you were born, I set you apart, I knew you from your mother's womb" (Jer 1:5). Later, the Lord speaks the same word to John the Baptist (Lk 1:15), of Christ (cf. Is 49) and of Paul (Gal 1:15). These words that are spoken to Jeremiah are also spoken to us since we are not products of chance but are called from all eternity to know Christ and to share His divine grace and plan for the salvation of the world (cf. Eph 1).

The word Jeremiah speaks is the word of authority, to uproot and pull down, to destroy and overthrow, to build and to plant. This is really the mission of all who work in the Lord's vineyard because there can be no compromise between authentic faith and the way the Christian life is lived. Often the genuine apostle/prophet must destroy in order to build.

Isaiah's call (6:1-13) took place in the form of a vision, a brief moment in which he encounters the Lord God in an intimate, authentic way. This encounter marked him for his whole life, for he had touched and had been touched by the mystery, the holiness and the power of God. As Isaiah, in the presence of the Holy One, experienced that he was unclean, so we too in the presence of the Living God experience that we are sinful, unworthy, incapable of placing ourselves in the hands of God who envelops us with His presence. In the moment of Isaiah's turning to the Lord, making his act of faith, he is cleansed interiorly through the fire of the Lord's love and Isaiah accepts completely the mission God offers him. Isaiah becomes God's spokesman.

Challenged by the word of God, many people and many social groups close themselves off, rejecting the message that could save them. The word of God is for our rising or our downfall, depending on how we welcome it in our hearts (Lk 2:34).

Jeremiah and Isaiah, two of the major prophets of the Old Testament, show us aspects of our call to be prophets in this twentieth century. Hearing God's invitation, we too can be aware of our sinfulness, unworthiness, lack of skill or vision, our inexperience. We can be frightened by the task set before us. We can be over-awed by the wonder, the holiness, the mystery of our God. We are challenged by the fact that our faith must be genuine, authentic, expressed in a life lived out in conformity with the will of God. We each have our word to speak to the world in which we live, a world hungry to hear the truth, a world in need of direction, a world that needs to be rebuilt, a world that must choose to respond to God's call—His invitation to walk in holiness, truth and justice.

If we do not respond to the responsibility that is ours as disciples of Christ Jesus, who will? You and I—we are called to be prophets today, to uproot and pull down, to destroy and overthrow, to build and to plant. Above all, our lived lives must conform to the will of the Living God so that we first live what we proclaim.

CHAPTER 9

PROPHECY: TO SPEAK FOR GOD

For the Hebrews of the Old Testament a prophet is one who is sent or one who is made to speak. Although biblical tradition traces the origins of Israelite prophecy to Moses (Num 11:24-30), not much is heard of the prophets until the late period of the judges and the early monarchy, when prophets are mentioned in connection with the Philistine wars. At this time they are shown stimulating, patriotic and religious fervour and are seen to be ecstatic prophets, those who lived and travelled in groups and prophesied from the ecstasy that resulted from dancing wildly to music.

The basic sources of what constitutes a prophet are found in the accounts of the call of the major prophets, Isaiah, Jeremiah, Ezekiel and Amos. The stories of the call of these prophets show us that the prophet is delegated to speak on behalf of Yahweh (Is 6:8-9), that the prophetic vocation is compelling even though the prophet is reluctant or lacking in talent (Amos 3:7-8, Jer 1:4-19), and that God communicates His word to the prophet (Is 6:9, Jer 1:7-9 and Ezek 2:8-3:3). We are also told that this communication involves mind and auditory experiences.

In the Old Testament the role of the prophet is seen in the light of the one God who chose the people of Israel from among all the nations and communicated His Will to His chosen people in the Law. The prophets foretold judgment and salvation for the people, criticized empty forms of worship and called the people of Israel to their social and religious responsibilities.

The New Testament gives abundant evidence to the fact that there were prophets in the early Christian communities. In spite of the fact that there were "charismatic leaders" in the New Testament, prophecy became submerged in the development of the hierarchical offices of the Church at the end of the first century.

Even so, prophecy in our day is a gift for the building up of the Body of Christ, the Church, in order that the Church may once again become a more powerful and influential force in the world. The greatest need in our own times is the recovery of the New Testament Church life. Prophecy is used both to foretell and to forth-tell. However, to speak forth the mind of God is the sense in which it is used most in our day, in order to encourage, admonish and re-affirm the people of God. Who can prophesy? Anyone whom the Lord chooses to use. Let us remember that is it given to a member of the Body of Christ for the common good of the Church. It is not an ability given to someone to prophesy at will but rather a definite message given at a particular time by the Spirit for a distinct purpose.

Prophecy has as its main function to edify, to build up or strengthen the Church. Among its other purposes are encouragement, consolation, teaching, prediction and conviction. Prophets too are always to be in control both of themselves and of the message they speak. Those who hear prophecies should listen to what is said (1 Cor 14:31) and all should weigh or discern what is said (1 Cor 14:29). It is necessary to discern the message that is spoken, not necessarily to accept everything that is said as "gospel-truth." If the Church is to grow, the people must be edified not only by good deeds but by the spoken word. When the word spoken is of the Spirit, those who hear the Word of prophecy have a witness within themselves as to the truth or error of the word spoken.

In testing prophecy there are some points to look at: the conformity of the word to Scripture, the context of love in which it is spoken, the tone of voice and the words of the speaker and whether or not it edifies those who hear the word. Does it help or strengthen the listener? Is it consistent with the Spirit and character of Jesus and does it witness to the Holy Spirit? If the prophecy "foretells," does it come to pass?

There is no individual who can discern correctly all the time. Hence, shared judgment is very important. It would be good to have someone or a team of people, recognized by the prayer groups, who could take a responsibility to care for, encourage, and correct those who exercise prophetic gifts. Usually, the best choice of persons here would be leaders within the group or those who have matured in the exercise of the gift themselves. Correction must be gentle, clear, and constructive. Discussions about prophecy should be done lovingly, with a desire to build up and encourage and never to tear down or hurt. Prophets always seem, in my experience, to be very sensitive people.

The prophetic word must become more evident and active in our lives and in the prayer groups to which we belong. Many groups today restrict the exercise of the gift because they seek only the clear exercise of the prophetic ministry. The right balance must be found in the use of the gift by those with a well-developed gift and those who are only beginning in the gift. St. Paul says it should be the most common gift (1 Cor 14:3). Patience is a real key in the growth towards maturity. As we gain maturity and experience, the Lord can speak more powerfully and clearly through us and others.

Let us discover in our own openness to the word of prophecy a real opportunity to learn from each other that we all have the responsibility to speak out the word of truth. Jesus is the prophet! Let us learn from Him.

CHAPTER 10

THE GIFT OF PROPHECY

Prophecy is a wonderful gift for building up the Christian assembly gathered in prayer. It is an anointed communication from God to an individual or a group of believers to give encouragement, reproof, inspiration or guidance. Above all, prophecy is a "forth-telling" of the mind and heart of God to His people. It may also foretell the future and is recognized as accurate when the word spoken comes to pass. St. Paul tells us to "seek the gifts, especially prophecy" (1 Cor 14:1).

The role of the prophet is to be a spokesperson for God. A prophet is not a prophet because of what he says—but because of his relationship with God. Not all who prophesy are prophets (cf. 1 Cor 14:31). Only some have the call to be prophet. A prophet is a person who consistently expresses prophetic words which are powerful and which elicit a response from many in the group. Their word has an impact, and consistently moves heart and spirit. It is important to examine a person's personal life in this regard—their relationship with God and conformity of life to His standards. All can prophesy, but only those who have been tested and tried in the furnace—who have faced the Cross over time— should be recognized as prophets. This may be a period of years. So don't quickly give the title of "prophet" to anyone.

Prophecy gives encouragement and strength in our weakness, corrects our sins, calls us to account, draws us closer to God in worship, and stirs up a response in God's people such as joy, freedom, peace, tranquillity, excitement, enthusiasm, and willingness to give all to the Lord. Guidance in our daily walk is another purpose for this gift.

Prophecy is a normal part of prayer group gatherings and it should be encouraged and sought on a regular basis. Prophecies come in three ways: sometimes the speaker receives the entire message, or a few words, or the sense of the prophetic word only. This is accompanied by what is called an "anointing" that varies from person to person. It may be tingling up and down the spine, a warm feeling all over, a racing of the heart. In some way, the Lord makes his presence felt, at least in the early stages of exercising the gift; but this often, in time, gives way to just knowing you have to speak. A message, together with the anointing or the certitude, would be a clear indication that one should speak the word they have been given.

It is important to look for the "now word" of the Lord. Prophecy is serious; it is the Lord's word to His people in a particular moment, in a particular set of circumstances. It is important to respond to the Holy Spirit's promptings, to speak in a way that people can understand—not in old English or in an emotionally distractive way—but simply, clearly, and loudly enough to be heard by all.

The word should be spoken in the right place and time and be for the group being addressed. Sometimes people tend to take the counsel or direction the Lord is giving to them personally, and apply it to the group. Always, it is the group addressed that is to discern the word, to recognize if indeed it is God's word to them at that particular time.

Our prophesying is imperfect because it comes through human intermediaries. But practice develops the gift and the quality of its delivery. All prophecy needs to be tested and discerned for its clarity and the fact that it is in tune with Scripture and Church teaching. Does it bear fruit? What about the life of the prophet? Is the prophet living the message s/he speaks? To test the Spirit we need to check the tone of the prophecy—whether given in love or hatred or anger—check that it makes common sense and that it glorifies the Lord Jesus Christ.

Prophecy can take many forms. It may be a prophetic oracle, given in the first or third person. It may be prophetic exhortation in which the Lord is encouraging, reviving, renewing or strengthening His people. It may be inspired prayer, or prophecy in song. Revelation may be one of the forms, but a caution enters here because it may be false (people can be wrong); it is not always appropriate to tell others, "The secrets of the heart are disclosed; then, falling on his face, he will have to worship God and declare that God is among you" (1 Cor 14:24-25). Personal prophecy is possible, given by one person to another, as well as having prophecy in personal prayer.

Another form would be describing a vision and its meaning. Prophetic actions are also a way of prophesying. The interpretation of tongues may also be prophetic, though it is most often inspired prayer giving worship and praise to God. Prophecy may also take the form of prophetic preaching or teaching.

Inspired Scripture reading is another form and is the most commonly exercised form of the word gifts. "All scripture is inspired by God and is useful for teaching, refuting error, for correcting and training in holiness so that the man of God may be fully competent and equipped for every good work (2 Tim 3:16-17). Not all Scriptures are to be read aloud. Discernment is needed. Who is it for? Does it fit? A common error is to read too long a passage so that the main point of the reading is missed or ignored. In reading, try to discern the key verses first. Proper discernment must be followed before taking action on a word. There should be a consistent, clear repetition of the message over a period of time and the word must be received by reliable members of the prayer group. There should be confirmation of the word through other word gifts and guidance should be sought from responsible leaders. Of course, it must be in tune with Scripture and Church teaching. This discernment applies especially where a major change of direction is involved.

One way to help people to develop this gift is to teach on it and invite people to respond to what Jesus would say to them or this particular group if He were physically standing before them. The response would be words like: "Do not be afraid," "I am with you," "Peace," "I love you," "Follow me," "We need to talk." People are often afraid to speak out before a large group, so I find it helpful, then, to divide them into small groups of six to eight, encourage them to hold hands, pray in tongues, and then ask the Lord to stir up the Spirit and give each a word to speak. After they have shared the word in the small groups, I would ask for each group to share a summary of the word spoken in their group. This is one way to develop the exercise of the gift in the prayer group, and may be repeated for several weeks until the group is comfortable in speaking out the word.

Some final thoughts: walk with the word you speak and walk in humility and contrition. Maintain a teachable spirit. Jesus always listened to the voice of the Father. Be sensitive to the mood of the Spirit, whether calm, joy, praise, etc. Walk always under authority; then you may speak in authority. We have to wait on the Lord; it takes a lot of time for God to fulfill His word in people. Do not become judgmental; God still is the one who does the judging. When you walk under authority you put to death the spirit of independence. It is not your task to fulfill the word; it is God's. You are just to deliver it in the way God wants. Keep your spirit pure. Forgive, clear up the past. No wrong motivation is permitted in the Lord's prophet. Avoid prophetic competition. Prophets do speak to real issues in the Church, to concrete situations. Always build up; don't tear down. Do not try to control others with your prophecy. Be careful about exposing the sins of others publicly. Catch God's vision and proclaim it in love.

CHAPTER 11

DISCERNMENT OF SPIRITS

Discernment is a distinguishing, a separation between options and is defined by Webster's dictionary as: "the quality of being able to grasp and comprehend what is obscure." Discernment of spirits is a revelational gift like prophecy, tongues and interpretation, word of wisdom, or word of knowledge. These are gifts by which God makes known something about the present situation to His people. This gift of the Spirit allows a person to distinguish between spirits, to tell whether an evil spirit is at work in a person or situation, or whether it is the Holy Spirit, or simply is it just a person's own spirit. It also could be a combination of spirits or forces at work.

The discernment can take place through a vision or a sense. I remember years ago, shortly after the Bread of Life Prayer Community began, a man came to the meeting and began to expound false teaching—that our baptism was not valid unless we had been fully immersed in water. As I looked around the room, I visibly, in vision, saw everyone in the room lifting off their chairs in indignation. Sensing what was being revealed by the Spirit I intervened and brought closure to his remarks and presented the correct teaching.

The spiritual gift of discernment of spirits must not be confused with a critical spirit on the natural level. It is too easy to judge the motives of another. Sometimes keen insight into human nature, such as some people possess naturally, can be confused with this supernatural gift. This gift has to do with the discerning of "spirits," not just of people in their purely natural courses of action.

This gift is a defence against deception. From its earliest stage the Church has and should have a constant experience of the supernatural in meetings, worship, and the daily life of the Church members. Satan is constantly working against the activities of the Holy Spirit and tries to counterfeit the wonderful works of God. So there is real danger in the possibility of deceiving spirits working great havoc. Many converts to the Church, and even members of the Church, have been steeped in paganism, spiritism, demon possession, New Age, or a whole variety of teaching that is contrary to the action of the Holy Spirit.

The discernment of spirits is both defensive and offensive, recognizing what spirit is at work through the human channel and acting on the recognition so that the person or situation is delivered through the power of the name of the Lord Jesus Christ.

Unspiritual or prejudiced people can cause real harm by judging or condemning a real work of God because it does not conform to their personal standards of just how God should manifest His power. Spiritual things can only be spiritually discerned. Thus, this gift can operate only in and through the spiritual person, not in a carnal believer. To discern is to pierce through all that is merely outward and see right through the person or situation so that God's light is revealed.

People often tend to criticize what they don't understand; for example, Baptism in the Holy Spirit, being slain or overwhelmed in the Spirit, the gift of tears, the Father's blessing, speaking in tongues. Those who judge the baptism and gifts of the Holy Spirit are wrong if they have not experienced them as part of their walk in the Lord. The New Testament gives certain standards for the discernment process: judge by the fruits (Mt 7:15-23); able to proclaim Jesus is Lord only in the power of the Spirit (1 Cor 12:3); those who are of God listen to Him (1 Jn 4:1-6). These tests are open to all believers and do not imply possession of any particular gift of the Holy Spirit.

Jesus clearly discerns the spirit in Nathaniel, Nicodemus, the woman of Samaria, with all people (Jn 2:25). In Scripture we see the gift evident in Joseph, David, Solomon, Elisha, Peter and Paul. This gift reveals the true nature of the source of any supernatural manifestation, whether it is divine or satanic, whether it is to be accepted or rejected, relied upon or resisted. There should be a powerful witness within but also an actual revelation of the Spirit at work. It takes great grace to balance the possession of such a gift and even greater grace to exercise it to the glory of God.

It is good to remember that discernment is for the guidance of others, rarely for oneself. Good and evil spirits are recognizable by their fruits. Authentic gifts are those that edify the Church, and bring improvement, growth or unity to the Body of Christ. The Spirit reveals Himself by powerful signs, miracles, the certitude of expressing God's word and meeting with persecution. Authentic gifts are marked by peace, light and fraternal charity. The supreme criterion of discernment is found in one's attitude in relation to Jesus Christ. Jesus Christ is Lord. There is no other!

CHAPTER 12

THE MINISTRY OF DELIVERANCE

"The seventy-two returned in jubilation saying, 'Master, even the demons are subject to us in your name.' He said in reply: 'I watched Satan fall from the sky like lightning. See what I have done; I have given you power to tread on snakes and scorpions and all the forces of the enemy, and nothing shall ever injure you. Nevertheless, do not rejoice so much in the fact that the devils are subject to you as that your names are inscribed in heaven'" (Lk 10:17-20).

I firmly believe that the more time we give to the enemy, the less we are giving to the Lord. But it is necessary to know your enemy, his tactics, his ways of operating, his tricks and ways of thinking, if we are to stand strong and resist his advances and attacks.

To live a life of grace and obedience to the will of the Lord, while being awake and watchful, wearing the full armour of God, puts one in the right place before the Lord.

Discerning of spirits is a most necessary gift given to the Church, and the Christian who exercises the gift supernaturally perceives something that is taking place in the spirit world, as Jesus would have discerned it. To discern, one must recognize what force is at work. Is it the Holy Spirit, the evil spirit, or the human spirit? To know the Lord, to know the enemy and to know yourself (and others) makes the process of discernment of spirits an easy one. Some examples of discernment found in the Scriptures are: Micaiah and the lying spirit (1 Kg 22:19-23), Jesus and the demoniac (Mk 5:1-20), and Paul and the fortune teller (Ac 16:16-18).

In the Charismatic Renewal the practice of many people is to offer prayers for deliverance. Commonly, this is done by saying a certain formula of prayer, one of the most popular being the "Prayer to take Authority." This kind of prayer is used by many, time and time again, even in the presence of the Blessed Sacrament, to cast out Satan and any sign or trace of his power from the place where the believer or the prayer gathering takes place. Others will do the same thing by sprinkling holy water or blessed salt around the area of meeting. Others pray the prayer to St. Michael the Archangel. Another way that is extremely effective is simply to invite people to focus on the Lord and then to pray in tongues until the whole community is free and deeply aware of the presence of the Lord Jesus.

To pray a prayer of deliverance is a good thing to do, but it is not the prayer itself that has the power but rather the faith of the individual(s) who speaks out, inviting the Lord Jesus to be present and to move in power. The enemy always flees when we resist him. A prayer can become part of a ritual action that loses its power or meaning in time. What is important is one's focus upon the Lord, and that focus gives life, power and authority. James 5:16 tells us: "The fervent petition of a holy man is powerful indeed."

We are called to walk with God, liberated from sin by following the Spirit. Righteousness comes from walking with the Spirit in holiness of life. When we walk with God our mentality changes, from flesh to Spirit; we are totally at peace by being spiritually minded or focused. By walking with God we are healed, receiving the fullness of life in God, intimacy with the Father of all, and the strength to die to self.

God must be able to trust us with His power and we have to trust God that He will minister freedom and healing through the simple word command spoken in His name. The Christian believer must put on strength—spiritual strength against temptation, sin and Satan—in order that weakness will go. He must put on garments of holiness and righteousness so that sin will have no place in his life. He must no longer have fellowship with the wicked so that he does not fall into uncleanness and rebellion. As he puts on strength in the way of the Lord he will loose himself from the grip of the Evil One and the sins that keep coming back upon him.

The person who enters into deliverance ministry must strive to be holy, humble, obedient, loving and yielded to the Lord. S/he must be a person of prayer. Those who enter this ministry without the strength of personal prayer will become oppressed, go back into the world, be taken away like slaves, will weep and wail, caught in bondage. Because they do not awake, they will sell themselves to the devil for nothing and they will be found among the wicked who blaspheme God. This can happen to Christians who do not pray (cf. Is 52:3-5). It is a serious matter to enter into deliverance ministry.

Any Christian can withstand the enemy by the power of God. He can resist temptation, telling the enemy to be gone in Jesus' name. Any Christian can offer prayer for protection from the enemy. But only those Christians who are people of prayer, striving for holiness, living in the presence of the Lord while bringing their lives into subjection to Jesus, should enter when called by the Lord into deliverance ministry. Otherwise, confusion can result and great harm be done.

Deliverance ministry refers specifically to setting people free who are bound by the power of evil, either through obsession, bondage, or partial possession. Exorcism is reserved to the power of the Church with the authority of the bishop invested in a particular priest for the freeing from full possession of a trapped soul; and only after every other possibility is considered can this work be done.

Usually, deliverance ministry is accomplished easily, quietly and simply in conjunction with the inner healing ministry. When the hold of sin is far stronger than the person can handle, when the person is obsessed with certain evil thought processes and can't break free, when the person needs help to resist the devil and gain back control in his life, then deliverance ministry can be called for. Also, deliverance is frequently and quietly done by simple command of the priest in the course of the Sacrament of Reconciliation.

When we view ourselves as a walled city and we see that the enemy has gained a foothold or control of a certain area of the city by coming through an area of the wall that is poorly defended, then we see that the enemy needs to be expelled and the defenses strengthened. This is the area of deliverance ministry. When control of the city has been taken over completely, this is the area for exorcism.

The Lord has invested tremendous power in us for our own blessing and the blessing of His people. Let's respect that power and authority and use it wisely and well for the Lord's glory and the ongoing blessing of His people. Let's move in the Lord's anointing and timing for then this ministry is most effective, especially in the strength of holiness and prayer.

Deliverance ministry has become very visible in the Church through the Charismatic Renewal. In an age when the power of God is more and more evident, we also see the concurrent rise of evil as we work to establish the reign of our God on earth as it is in heaven.

CHAPTER 13

THE GIFT OF TONGUES

It was November 1971. At the prayer meeting a woman asked us to pray that she receive the gift of Tongues—the ability and freedom to pray in a language she had never learned. We prayed, but she didn't receive. I did. A few months before, I had been prayed with to receive the Baptism in the Holy Spirit. Then, when I didn't expect it, I received the gift of Tongues. It was the most ecstatic experience of my life. The woman who did not receive that night received the following Good Friday evening, together with her husband and two children. The Lord reserved a special blessing for her.

To pray, to speak or sing in Tongues is to pray in what could be an earthly or heavenly language; a language current on the earth or one long dead, or it could be any one of countless dialects. Tongues is a spontaneous, inspired utterance by the Holy Spirit in which we use our voice according to the Spirit's prompting. To speak or sing in Tongues or "to pray in the Spirit," as it's called, is what happens when a believer allows the indwelling Spirit to guide and form the words he/she utters. "All of them began to speak in other tongues as the Spirit enabled them" (Ac 2:4).

This gift is not necessarily a sign of being filled with the Spirit, nor do people filled with the Spirit necessarily exercise this gift. Yet everyone who wants it could yield to the gift, since it is present in everyone who believes and is filled with, or baptized, in the Holy Spirit. The Spirit indwells with every gift; and many, many people use this gift in their prayer time either when alone or with others.

Frequently enough, a speaker in Tongues will have several different prayer Tongues and will use them at different times. For example, praying in petition will involve one Tongue, singing in the Spirit another, praise and worship another, deliverance ministry another. Sometimes people experience that their prayer language will change periodically, maybe every few months. This happens more so when people regularly use their gift of Tongues.

There are three basic ways in which Tongues are manifested. One, from the day of Pentecost, where the utterance in Tongues is not understood by the speaker, but when overheard by the public and without interpretation, is understood by those whose own language it is. "How is it that each of us hears them in his own native language?" (Ac 2:4-8). Another is the use of Tongues in public worship. The language used is not known and should be followed by an interpretation through the prompting of the Holy Spirit (cf. 1 Cor 14:27). Still, another is the use of Tongues in private which needs no interpretation, though this could be requested in prayer (1 Cor 14:13).Those who exercise Tongues in public do so in private.

What is the purpose of Tongues? The main purpose is for edification, whether done privately or in public (Jude 20, 21; 1 Cor 14:4-5). A Tongue is addressed to God and is used for praise. We can describe it as a love language when one is lost in wonder, love, or praise and human words are inadequate or exhausted to express our inner feelings. "We hear them declaring the wonders of God in our own tongues" (Ac 2:11). "For they heard them speaking in tongues and praising God" (Ac 10:46).

Praying in Tongues also sets off the other word gifts of the Spirit such as prophecy, interpretation, word of knowledge and word of wisdom. Tongues used in public worship enables the Church to function as a body. One speaks, another gives the interpretation (not translation), and others are blessed by the interpretation. In the case of Tongues with interpretation, where the Tongue is not understood by the speaker, but understood by an unbelieving bystander, it is meant to be a sign of the Kingdom of God (1 Cor 14:22; Ac 2:12).

Tongues expresses a verbal intimacy with God, providing a whole new dimension in a person's prayer life. This prayer of Tongues is an intimate prayer language that may be used in times of joy, pain, fear, grief, searching or hungering to draw closer to the Lord. Only God understands what we are praying, since the Spirit within us is praying—although we know the sense of the prayer, whether it is praise, intercession, deliverance ministry or addressing the spirit of another when praying over another. "We do not know what we ought to pray, but the Spirit himself intercedes for us with groans and utterances that words cannot express" (Rom 8:26).

Praying in Tongues brings deliverance, inspiration, refreshment (both spiritually and physically), revival, wisdom and is a means to victory in spiritual warfare, whether during times of personal conflict or when in ministry to others in the areas of deliverance or exorcism. St. Paul strongly encourages us to pray in the Spirit on all occasions with all kinds of prayer and requests (Eph 6:18) when he speaks of the spiritual warfare in which we are involved.

This gift is often initially received at the time a person is baptized in the Holy Spirit. But it is not unusual that it is received at a later time as one grows in freedom and closeness to the Lord. When one is relaxed, free from tension, with an open heart and desire to praise or bless God, the gift is frequently released. The biggest block to praying in Tongues initially is "head knowledge," in that a person is responding to the Lord from their head (intellect), rather than from their heart. Sometimes people are afraid of appearing foolish, or just don't understand the why of Tongues, which is a yielding of control of the tongue over to the Lord. This gift can occur spontaneously when one is alone, or in prayer with a group who are praying or singing in Tongues; or can be released by requesting it from the Lord as one receives the laying on of hands in prayer.

Great joy or ecstasy may accompany the initial release of this gift. There is an act of the will necessary on the part of the individual to exercise this gift, both in starting to speak and in stopping, just as it would be for speech in any language. Often recipients will at first have only a few words, but as they continue to pray the gift will increase, just as a baby learns to talk and develop speech.

In private, this gift may be used anywhere—at work, driving, in the dentist's chair or the doctor's office. For example, it can be a great aid in regulating blood pressure and in removing tension, bringing peace, freedom and joy. It's good to have a specific time for prayer each day in Tongues, to pray out loud if possible because that strengthens the gift and one's confidence in exercising it. To pray in Tongues silently is one way of being continually in prayer.

When the gift of Tongues with interpretation is done in public, it is important to speak loudly and clearly for all to hear. To exercise this gift in this way in a public assembly, a definite anointing is needed and the people addressed will have no doubt that God is communicating this gift in this way. It may be spoken or sung in a Spirit-led melody.

Sometimes people are concerned with the origin of the gift and are afraid the Tongues may be false (originating from their own spirit). It should be generally presumed, in this case, that it is by the inspiration of the Holy Spirit and not one's own spirit, since one would know if they were "making it up." Hearers can also discern easily if they are being addressed in an authentic Tongue or if the speaker is simply speaking or singing their own prayer to the Lord. There is also such a thing as false Tongues which originate from the evil one and would be evident because they are accompanied with anger and/or hatred. I have only experienced this once in over twenty years of dealing with people, so it should not be a major concern. However, we should always be open to proper discernment.

The gift of Tongues is a tremendous blessing for our spiritual lives with tremendous implications for the way in which we live. If you have the gift, thank God! If you don't yet exercise it, ask the Lord for it, eagerly desire it, praise and bless the Lord. Take your eyes off the gift and put them on Jesus as you continue to praise, and let the good Lord form His gift in you using your own gift of speech.

CHAPTER 14

INTERPRETATION OF TONGUES

To pray in Tongues is a wonderful gift of the Holy Spirit by which we praise, worship and glorify God. It is a gift by which we turn over control of our tongue to God so that it may be a blessing not only to us but for others. Frequently, this "gift" is given at the time one receives the grace or the Baptism in the Holy Spirit, though for many it may begin at a later time—for me it occurred three months after I was prayed with for the release of the Holy Spirit in my life while I was praying for someone else to receive the gift of Tongues.

We may use the gift of Tongues in private prayer, and we should be doing so, but we may also use it in community prayer with others. This is called "praying in the Spirit," or we may sing it with our own individual melody that God gives us and then we call it "singing in the Spirit."

Those who use this gift in private prayer may also use it to address the assembly in tongues, but then it needs interpretation. This would not be a translation but an interpretation giving the sense of the message. It should preferably be done by one other than the speaker in tongues; but if no one interprets, then the one who spoke in tongues should give the interpretation. Both are gifts of the Holy Spirit for our edification, growth, strengthening, upbuilding, encouragement, or for revelation. Usually, the interpretation of the tongues spoken will be to glorify God and His greatness, or it may be a message very like prophecy, though it is intended to capture the heart of the uninitiated or the unbeliever. For example, the heart of a person searching may be revealed, and they will recognize that, "yes, this is God."

This supernatural revelation through the Holy Spirit enables the one with the interpretation to communicate in the language of the listeners—the equivalent of what was spoken in tongues. It is important that the interpretation be given in order that the assembly may be edified and built up. If there is no interpretation, then the speaker in tongues is discouraged and may not continue to exercise the gift in other circumstances, while the assembly may question the validity or purpose of the tongues spoken. St. Paul says that the tongues must be interpreted (1 Cor 14:28), otherwise he forbids the continued use of tongues without an interpretation.

It is important that people understand the manifestation of the gift of Tongues when it is spoken in public through an individual's utterance in speech or song. When it is sung, it is very beautiful, touching the heart and stirring the spirit of the listeners.

God freely and sovereignly gives the gift to whomever He chooses. It may come in a variety of ways, similar to the length and style of the tongue spoken; or it may be completely different, expressed in longer or shorter words, as a vision, a sense, an inspired thought or a symbol in pictures. The person with the interpretation may receive it as if the person were speaking directly to them in their own language, or it may just be a phrase or a word that comes as the individual is speaking in tongues.

Of course, tongues used in private prayer to praise God does not need interpretation, nor does praying or singing in the Spirit, since each one is offering their praise or petition to God individually together in the group.

More than one person may be used to complete the interpretation, but there should not be several interpretations—especially if they are contradictory. When one addresses the assembly in tongues, the assembly should wait for or ask for the interpretation before moving on. Sometimes, people being given prophetic words may intervene before the interpretation is given. They should be encouraged to wait. And, of course, discernment is always necessary. St. Paul says: "Are you going to speak in Tongues? Let two or three, at most, speak, each in turn, and let one interpret what has been said" (1 Cor 14:27).

This gift, like all the manifestations or gifts of the Holy Spirit, needs to be encouraged and called forth. It's most worthwhile to study the gifts and invite the Holy Spirit to manifest his presence in a variety of ways. We need all the gifts of the Spirit. One is not more important than another, but all are necessary for revealing and building up the Kingdom of God. We need to be empowered for the ministry of service that we may share in the mission of Jesus as bearers of the Spirit without measure.

TO ORDER

Teaching Materials by Father Peter B. Coughlin

Books
• *Understanding the Charismatic Gifts*
• *The Fire in My Heart*
• *HE'S ALIVE!*

Video Cassette Packages
• Life in the Spirit Seminars
• The Charismatic Gifts of the Holy Spirit

Audio Cassettes
• Life in the Spirit Seminars
• Various Topics

For further reading on Life in the Spirit, subscribe to *The Bread of Life* magazine.

To order these materials or for more information, please contact:

C.C.S.O. Bread of Life Renewal Centre
P.O. Box 127
Burlington, Ontario L7R 3X8 Canada

www.thebreadoflife.ca

Telephone (905) 634-5433 or FAX (905) 634-1495

Notes